Simon Tugwel

Saint Dominic
and the
Order of Preachers

DOMINICAN PUBLICATIONS

This edition first published (2001) by
Dominican Publications, 42 Parnell Square, Dublin 1, Ireland
ISBN 1-871552-78-8
British Library Cataloguing in Publication Data.
A catalogue record for this book is available from the British Library.
Printed in Spain by Estudios Gráficos Zure.

The illustrations

On the cover and page 2, Saint Dominic at Fanjeaux, from a stained glass window in Fanjeaux, France, by Jean Hugo. Photograph by Austin Flannery, OP.

From *Modi Orandi Sancti Dominici*: Ways of Prayer of Saint Dominic, with kind permission: (i) 'St Dominic Meditating in Prayer', p 33, detail from the fifth way of prayer (ii) 'St Dominic Would Open Some Book', p 36, detail from the eighth way of prayer. *Modi Orandi Sancti Dominici* is an illuminated manuscript, in *Codex Rossianus 3*, which was painted and written between 1274 and 1280, possibly in northern Italy. It is now in the Vatican Library, Rome. The translations are by the late Leonard Boyle, OP, Prefect Emeritus of the Vatican Library.

By Albert Carpentier, OP: Saint Dominic Preaching, p 6; Saint Dominic's Encounter with an Inn-keeper, p 11; St Dominic Receives Women at Prouille, p 28. The last two pictures form part of a series of stained glass windows in a Dominican convent school, Sei Dominiko Gakuen, Setagaya-ku, Okamoto 1-10-1, Tokyo, Japan. Fr Carpentier, who has produced a large number of works of art on Dominican subjects, is director of the Fra Angelico Institute for Sacred and Liturgical Art, Tokyo. He lives in Sinju-ku, Hyakunin-cho, 2-23-27, 169-0073, Tokyo, Japan.

Saint Dominic disperses the Brothers, p. 19, by Sister Mary Grace Thul, OP, St Dominic's Monastery, 9401 16th Street, N.W., Washington, DC, 20001, U.S.A. Sr Mary Grace has exhibited in a number of American centres, has done illustrations and designed book covers for American publishers. She has done many illustrations for the forthcoming *St Dominic and His Family*, Dominican Publications, Dublin.

Saint Dominic at Prouille, p. 10, drawing by Sr Mary Ansgar Sheldon, OP, of a thirteenth century wooden sculpture at Prouille, France. A member of the Dominican Congregation of Saint Catherine of Siena, England, Sr Mary did many drawings and paintings, especially of Dominican subjects. She spent her final years in Bodø, Norway, where she died in 1995.

SAINT DOMINIC AT FANJEAUX

Legend has it that on three successive nights in July 1206 from the hill-town of Fanjeaux in southern France, St Dominic saw the Signadou, a globe of flame, come to rest over a ruined church in nearby Prouille.

Later he would know more clearly that his mission was to begin in southern France and that the nuns at Prouille and elsewhere were to be central to it.

Stained glass window by Jean Hugo, at Fanjeaux.

Chapter One

The Idea of the Order of Preachers

THE CHURCH, in the words of Psalm 44, has always been 'clothed in variety', not the least splendid aspect of which is the variety of her saints. Some become a kind of living image of holiness, attracting veneration during their life-time and becoming objects of cult as soon as they are dead. They leave behind them, in the imagination of succeeding ages, a vivid remembrance of what they were. The figure of St Francis, for instance, has haunted and inspired the church ever since he died in 1226.

Other saints are, as it were, more coy, and hide behind the works which live after them and the ideals which they prompted others to follow. Their individual personalities make less impression on the church's memory; like signposts, they point away from themselves. People may come to forget them as individuals, but they cannot escape for long from the ideas for which they stood.

St Dominic is one of the coy saints. When he died in 1221, the order which he had established, the Order of Preachers, commonly known as the Dominicans, buried him, sadly and affectionately, and then got on with the job he had given them. Unlike the Franciscans, they made no attempt to turn their founder into an object of cult; nor did they immediately start writing up his life to publicise his personal holiness. The earliest life that we have of Dominic is not called *A Life of St*

Dominic, but *A Little Book about the Beginnings of the Order of Preachers.*

In his life-time, Dominic had wished to be treated simply as one of the brethren, and his dying wish was that he should be buried beneath the feet of his brethren. It is quite in accordance with his own temperament that he should live on in the church, not as a striking individual, but in the work of preaching the gospel, for which his order came into being.

It is not surprising, then, that he has never been one of the popular favourites among the saints. Men and women do not keep returning to the thought of the man, Dominic, as they do to the thought of the man, Francis. It is rather to the idea of his order that they keep coming back. When the famous French preacher, Lacordaire, was campaigning for the restoration of the Dominican Order in France in 1839, he wrote: 'If God gave me the power to create a new order, I am convinced that, after much reflection, I should discover nothing more modern or better adapted to our time and its needs than the Rule of St Dominic. There is nothing antiquated about it except its history.'

Seven years later, Newman, wondering about his vocation as a Catholic, wrote: 'My present feeling is that what the world, or at least England, wants as much as anything, is Dominicans.' He was afraid that the Dominicans had, in fact, lost their tradition – all that he could discover about the Dominicans in Florence was that 'the said Dominicans were manufacturers of scented water etc., and had very choice wines in their cellar.' But, even if he feared that it was 'a great idea extinct', he could still say, 'The idea I like exceedingly.'

Since he wrote, it has become plain that the idea is far from extinct. The great revival of the Dominican Order in the nineteenth and twentieth centuries has given to the church some of its greatest theologians and preachers, men like M.J. Lagrange (the pioneer of Catholic biblical scholarship) and Yves Congar (one of the foremost theologians of Vatican II), and, in England and Ireland, some of the best loved Catholic preachers, such as Tom Burke, Vincent McNabb and Bede Jarrett. In 1970, Paul VI could echo the words of his predecessor, Gregory IX (who canonised St Dominic in 1234), and declare that the light which radiates from Dominic is a gift of providence for our times too.

SAINT DOMINIC PREACHING
By Albert Carpentier OP

Dominic was not primarily concerned to find a way of life which would be convenient or even safe for himself, nor was he concerned to realise any dream of his own perfection; what he wanted was to preach the gospel where it was needed most, in whatever way would make it most effective.

CHAPTER TWO

The Apostolic Life

'I DO NOT READ that Christ was a black monk or a white monk, but that he was a humble preacher.' With these words a thirteenth-century Dominican novice justified his choice of order against some monks who wished him to join them instead. The essential model to which St Dominic pointed in the thirteenth century was Christ himself, wandering round with 'nowhere to lay his head', proclaiming the kingdom of God; and Christ sent out his followers to do exactly the same. The church spread throughout the world because of the restless wandering of his preachers, and throughout the ages of Christian history we find people responding to the call of God in this way, leaving home and country, to travel round, bringing to all men and women the good news of Jesus Christ.

However, fashions in holiness, like fashions in clothes, change from time to time, and during the Middle Ages a very different model had been taking shape, stressing rather the life of seclusion and stability. The great Benedictine family of monks and nuns was increasingly seen as the essential pattern of holiness for men and women who sought to give their lives totally to God. The Benedictine way of life provided a context in which a spiritual life could develop peacefully, in the discipline of the cloister, far removed from many of the temptations of normal life, and freed from the distractions and tensions inherent in any active apostolate. The perfection of monastic observance came to be seen as the closest approximation on earth to the regime of paradise.

Then the fashion began to change again. In the twelfth century a number of devout Christians began to feel a longing for a simpler, less organised, less secure life, more obviously modelled on the gospels. But their aspirations, on the whole, found no easy expression in the church of the time, and many of them fell foul of ecclesiastical authority. Some of them, for whatever reasons, separated themselves altogether from the church and began to preach strange doctrines.

By the beginning of the thirteenth century, there was a major crisis in some parts of Europe, particularly in the South of France, where a fully-fledged anti-church existed, committed to the dualist doctrine that the material world is evil and that it was made, not by God, but by an evil anti-God.

The problem was complicated by the failure, by and large, of most of the bishops and priests to present true Christian doctrine in an attractive and convincing way, or even to present it at all. The heretics found it easy to score points against the official church, because the clergy were often not setting a very good example of Christian living; it was difficult for people to recognise in them the authentic successors of the apostles.

What was urgently needed was for the church to show that the religious aspirations of the people could be met within the church, and to proclaim in an informed and sensitive way the genuine gospel of Christ.

In different ways both St Dominic and St Francis responded

to this need. Both men adopted a way of life similar to that which the various heretical groups had adopted, a life of utter poverty and dependence on God's providence, an adventurous life in the world, not hidden away in monastic seclusion, a life of devotion to active service of others; in addition, Dominic set himself to preach and to attract others to preach, and he was concerned that he and his preachers should know their faith thoroughly and be able to expound it competently.

In a striking phrase, Dante describes St Dominic as *l'amoroso drudo della fede cristiana* which may be roughly translated as 'the boyfriend of the Christian faith.' If Francis was in love with his 'Lady Poverty', Dominic was in love with the Christian faith. His overwhelming desire was to bring to everybody the truth of the faith, which would set them free and save their souls. While he was still quite a young man, he had prayed insistently and passionately that God would give him true charity which would be effective in procuring the salvation of others, and he longed to spend himself totally in the service of the gospel, just as Christ had given himself even to death for the salvation of the world.

Dominic was not primarily concerned to find a way of life which would be convenient or even safe for himself, nor was he concerned to realise any dream of his own perfection: what he wanted was to preach the gospel where it was needed most in whatever way would make it most effective.

The best way to preach the gospel in his own time, as he appreciated, was to imitate the manner of the apostles. Dominic never doubted for a moment that a preacher needed to be appointed by the church, but he saw no reason why an official preacher should behave like a secular potentate. He deliberately refused, as far as he could, any position which would set him above others and give him power over them. In his view, the preacher comes before his audience as a beggar, begging from God the word he is to speak, begging from men the bread which will keep him alive. Many of the clergy and religious had become entangled in secular affairs through their economic rights and responsibilities, which meant that, not only were they distracted from their concentration on the gospel, they often found themselves engaged in protracted conflict with their people. Dominic cut himself free from all that. He rediscovered one of the basic reasons why poverty and chastity are practised in the church: it is so that men and women can be free to devote themselves wholeheartedly and unambiguously to the Lord and to the work of the gospel.

He also realised that the gospel can be stifled by spiritual, as well as material, security. The monastic orders were very conscious of human frailty, and set up a great many prudential measures to protect people from themselves. But, if the risk of going astray is too thoroughly eliminated, the adventure of true charity can be lost too. Dominic re-affirmed the value of adventure, beckoning to generous hearts and minds to come out, as Abraham came out, and follow the uncharted paths of obedience to God, relying on God's protection and the help of Our Lady rather than on their own prudence.

During the celebrations of the eighth centenary of Dominic's birth, Cardinal Villot described him as a man who was 'stupefyingly free', and the spirit of freedom is deeply stamped on the Dominican tradition. It comes from taking the risk of trusting in God and trusting in the generosity of other people, whoever they may be.

Drawing of the thirteenth century sculptured head of Dominic at Prouille, France, by Sr Mary Ansgar Sheldon, op, member of the (English) congregationof St Catherine of Siena (Stone), who died in 1995 at the age of 87.

SAINT DOMINIC'S ENCOUNTER WITH AN INN-KEEPER

On their way to the north, Dominic and Diego spent a night at Toulouse, where their landlord turned out to be a supporter of the dualist anti-church of the Albigensians. Dominic's reaction is revealing. He sat up all night arguing with him, and eventually convinced him of the truth of the Catholic faith.

From a stained glass window in a Dominican convent in Tokyo, Japan, by Albert Carpentier, OP.

Chapter Three

The Beginnings of the Order

EVEN IN THE thirteenth century, various dates were given for the beginning of the Dominican Order, and they are all suggestive in different ways.

The earliest proposed date is 1198, which is probably when Dominic became a canon of Osma, in Castile. The Bishop of Osma, Martín Bazán, needed good men for his cathedral chapter, and his attention was drawn to Dominic by a spectacular act of generosity. Dominic had been sent by his parents to Palencia, the first university in Spain; after doing the usual course in arts, he embarked on the study of theology. But, in response to a serious famine in the district, he sold his beloved books and his furniture and used the money to establish a regular provision of food for the starving. His example, we are told, inspired others to follow suit, and some of them later attached themselves to him when he became a preacher.

Acute sympathy for the distress of others remained a characteristic of Dominic throughout his life, and he was prepared to adopt extreme measures to relieve their distress. Once he even offered to sell himself into slavery to obtain the ransom of someone held captive by the Moors. But his sympathy did not simply spend itself in extravagant gestures; he realised the importance of giving institutional form to his generosity. Our information is quite precise, that he 'established an almonry' in Palencia; even as a young man, he had the instincts of an organiser.

The immediate result of his generosity to the poor was that he caught the eye of Bishop Martín and the prior of his chapter, Diego. They persuaded Dominic to join them and so it was that, in about 1198, he became a canon of Osma.

There he learned about life in a religious community, and had an opportunity to pursue his theological studies and to devote himself to public and private prayer. He made such an impression on his fellow canons that by 1201 he had been appointed subprior. But even then he was yearning to sacrifice himself for the salvation of others. Although we have no reason to think he was unhappy as a canon, his true vocation lay elsewhere.

The first step towards his discovery of the distinctive task to which God was calling him came in 1203, another date suggested for the beginning of the Order. Diego, now Bishop of Osma, was sent by the King of Castile on an embassy to the Marches of Denmark (the part of northern Germany which was then under Danish rule), to negotiate a marriage for the Infante. Diego took Dominic with him. We may surmise that the two men had become friends and that Dominic was not just part of the bishop's retinue.

On their way to the North, they spent a night at Toulouse, where their landlord turned out to be a supporter of the dualist anti-church of the Albigensians. Dominic's reaction is revealing: he sat up all night arguing with him, and eventually persuaded him of the truth of the Catholic faith.

After successfully accomplishing their mission in the North, Diego and Dominic returned home; but almost immediately they were sent off again, with a larger retinue, to fetch the lady to consummate the marriage. In the meantime, however, she had died.

Bishop Diego, like Dominic, was distressed to discover how many people in the South of France were being led astray into heresy; on one occasion, he tried to preach to them, but the heretics just laughed at him. How could he, travelling like a prince, claim to be an apostle of Jesus Christ? But what moved him even more was what he heard about the Cumans. Some soldiers from this pagan people had been brought into Germany as mercenaries and there they had run amok, causing devastation wherever they went.

Instead of returning to Osma, Diego and his companions went to see the pope, and Diego asked for permission to resign his see, so that he could go and preach to the Cumans; presumably Dominic was included in his plans. But the pope refused Diego's request and told him to return to his diocese. And this Diego did, but not without a major adventure on the way.

While he and his party were passing through the South of France, in March or April 1206, they met the legates appointed by the pope to combat heresy in the region – the Abbot of Cîteaux (Arnaud Amalric) and two other Cistercians. These unfortunate monks had met with little but failure, and they had gathered at Montpellier to consider whether they should not abandon their mission, or at least abandon their preaching and try to reform the clergy first, whose bad example was one of the heretics' main assets. When Diego unexpectedly arrived, they asked his advice.

To their amazement, Diego, who had learned from his own experience of the heretics, proposed that, far from abandoning their preaching, they should concentrate on it. And, to combat the propaganda of the heretics, they should reform, not the clergy, but themselves. They should adopt a style of life in exact imitation of the apostles – which would, of course, also mean imitating the heretics. As Diego realised, the great advantage that the heretical preachers had was their austere, evangelical appearance; they *looked* like apostles. The best way to oppose them would be to show that Catholics could be equally austere and evangelical. They too should travel on foot, in poverty and humility, begging their bread from door to door, spreading the true gospel of Jesus Christ. Why not?

There were, of course, plenty of reasons why not. It was, for one thing, considered improper for senior churchmen to beg, and it was, in particular, considered unbecoming for Cistercians to beg – only the very next year a Swiss monastery was threatened with closure if its monks could not support themselves without begging. And the whole enterprise of itinerant, mendicant preaching smacked of heresy in the eyes of many church leaders. Still, the three papal legates agreed that they would give the new method a try, provided someone respectable gave them a lead.

Diego accepted the challenge without hesitation. He sent his retinue home, keeping only Dominic with him, and set off, on foot, to proclaim the gospel.

Diego himself soon returned to his diocese, in obedience to

the pope's orders. But by his bold gesture he had launched a new style of Catholic preaching; and he continued to help in any way he could. In collaboration with the Cistercian Bishop of Toulouse, Fulk of Marseilles, a former troubadour, he began to set up staging-posts to serve as centres for a systematic campaign of preaching throughout the region; the most important of these, perhaps the only one he succeeded in erecting, was at Prouille, where he also established a community of nuns. He returned to the region more than once, and took part in several public debates with the heretics; after one of them, we are told, 150 people returned to the church, and one participant commented that he had never imagined the Catholics had such strong arguments to support their position, which shows how ignorant people were of Catholic doctrine.

Most significantly, as soon as the pope authorised the recruitment of extra preachers, Diego seconded Dominic to the mission, together with some other canons, two or three of whom remained with Dominic to become founding members of the Order of Preachers. Later Dominicans were not wrong to see these events as an important beginning of the Order.

Various preachers came and went, but Dominic, with his small band of companions, persevered through nearly ten years, preaching, arguing, making friends, and generally showing that the heretics had no monopoly on evangelical prowess. There were some spectacular successes, and some less spectacular. We know of several individual conversions, and there were probably others which have left no mark on history. But the preaching was not allowed to develop in peace for very long, and, by the end of 1207, two of its main protagonists were dead: the papal legate most involved in the new campaign, and Diego himself.

In January 1208, one of the remaining legates was assassinated by the heretics; it was suspected that the Count of Toulouse was implicated in the crime. As a result, Pope Innocent III lost patience and appealed to the King of France more insistently than ever to intervene militarily in the region, to restore order and orthodoxy. So, the following year, began an ugly war which, after much suffering and bloodshed, resulted eventually in the absorption of the South into the kingdom of France; but it is far from clear to what extent it hastened the decline of heresy.

The death of Diego and the diversion of interest to the crusade meant that Dominic became the head of what was left of the preaching mission; he was also responsible for Prouille, which, under his guidance, developed into a proper nunnery, with a small community of clerics attached. As was normal in the period, no one saw any contradiction between peaceable attempts at conversion and the more violent methods of warfare; Dominic and the leader of the crusade (Simon de Montfort, the father of the one famous in English history) became friends, and Simon and other barons who were with him were valuable benefactors of Prouille and of the preachers. But Dominic never abandoned his own task; to the best of his ability, in spite of the horrors of war, he remained faithful to the apostolic work and the apostolic life which he had inherited from his bishop.

At the time of his death, Diego was hoping to get leave from the pope to collect some suitable people on whom to base a permanent preaching mission. Nothing came of it at the time, but Dominic and Fulk did their best to keep the idea alive. After the massive defeat of the heretics at the battle of Muret in 1214, things began to look more promising; the idea was revived of making Prouille a preaching base, not just a nunnery, and Dominic was given the nearby parish of Fanjeaux. In the outcome, though, it was in Toulouse that the dream became a reality. Early in 1215 Dominic was given a house there by a rich burgher, Peter Seilhan; even more importantly, Peter and another man, called Thomas, put themselves at Dominic's disposal by a kind of religious profession, and some others were attracted to join them. Bishop Fulk gave them the status of a preaching institute in his diocese, charged, not only with the mission against heresy, but with responsibility to assist in all the different facets of his doctrinal ministry. Thus Diego's apostolic vision, matured by Dominic's experience in the intervening years, acquired a stable embodiment in the community gathered round Dominic in Toulouse.

This was the situation when Dominic went with Fulk to the Fourth Lateran Council in late 1215. He was the superior of a body of men with a recognised status in the diocese as preachers in the manner of the apostles; its permanence was, in principle, assured by its right to recruit on its own account. But there was, of course, one flaw: there was no guarantee that any future bishop would permit it to continue. Dominic and

Fulk therefore wanted the pope to confirm their foundation, which they probably thought of as an 'order of preaching'.

Dominic and Fulk had, no doubt, been encouraged in their hopes and plans by a decree of the local Council of Avignon in 1209, calling on bishops to be more assiduous in preaching and inviting them to appoint other preachers to help them. An identical call for more preaching was on the agenda of Lateran IV, and the pope clearly realised that what Dominic had pioneered in Toulouse had implications for the church as a whole.

Innocent III had long been a supporter of the various apostolic movements which had been springing up, including a group of Waldensians who wished to return to the church after being converted by Diego; but he had been forced to acknowledge that local hierarchies, in general, did not welcome them. And he was not unaware of the dangers posed by fringe religious groups. Another item on the agenda, therefore, was a plan to secure the boundaries of religious life by requiring all new foundations to be made on the basis of one of the established Rules.

Innocent did not confirm Dominic's preaching institute in Toulouse. This is not because he was unsympathetic; on the contrary, he envisaged a role for Dominic's preachers far wider than anything that Dominic had ever dreamed of. He suggested that they should choose a recognised Rule and thus turn their diocesan institute into a religious order which could spread without limit. Since every religious house needed a church, Fulk willingly undertook to find them one. And the pope told Dominic that, if the preachers took the steps he had recommended he would give Dominic everything he wanted. Dominic was naturally dismayed at the gap between the paucity of his preachers and the immense prospect opening out before them; but he was reassured, we are told, by a vision of his brethren going out, two by two, into all the world to preach the gospel.

So Dominic returned to Toulouse early in 1216 with both a promise and a challenge far in excess of the hopes he had taken with him to Rome. The brethren chose to adopt the Rule of St Augustine, together with parts of the customary of the reformed order of canons, the Praemonstratensians. They prudently did not yet attempt to draft any legislation about their identity as preachers; they needed first to discover by experiment how to be both preachers and canons. Fulk gave them the church of Saint Romain in Toulouse, into which they moved; he also gave them two other churches in the diocese, which they were to staff when they could. Everything was set for Dominic to return to the pope and accept the confirmation that had been promised.

However significant the events of 1198, 1203, 1206 and 1215 may seem in retrospect, this is the real beginning of the order. It was in 1216 that the religious order came to birth which was to be known as the Order of Preachers.

SAINT DOMINIC DISPERSES THE BROTHERS

On 15 August he summoned the brethren and told them that they must split up without delay. A sizeable party was sent to Paris, including Bl. Bertrand of Garrigue, who had been prior of Saint Romain ... with instructions to establish a community there ... . At the same time four friars were sent to Spain to explore possibilities there.

Picture by Mary Grace Thul, OP

CHAPTER FOUR

The Development of the Order

THINGS DID NOT immediately work out as expected. Before Dominic could get back to Rome, Innocent died, and his successor, Honorius III, knew nothing of what had been planned. At first, all he would give Dominic, in December 1216, was a routine confirmation of Saint Romain as a house of canons. But Dominic worked patiently to convince him that they were something more than just canons; in January 1217 he received a remarkable letter recognising them as preachers in Toulouse.

He also obtained a letter addressed to the university of Paris, urging masters to uproot themselves from there and come to teach theology in Toulouse. Dominic had long appreciated that, in the campaign against heresy, it was not enough to look convincing as an apostle; it was also necessary to refute heresy by argument and to ensure that the Catholics had an informed faith with which to resist the allure of false doctrine. Preachers, in particular, had to be well instructed; that is why he had taken his first followers in Toulouse to the cathedral school, where an English master, Alexander Stavensby, was at the time lecturing on theology.

By the time he left Rome in 1217, Dominic had got what he had hoped to get in 1215, recognition of his brethren as diocesan preachers. But his own missionary yearnings had been re-awakened; he did not want to spend the rest of his life in

Toulouse. He made a deal with a young Italian nobleman, William of Monferrato, that in two years' time, after he had finished organising his order, they would set off together for the North to convert Prussians and other pagans; in the meantime, William would go and study in Paris.

Once again, though, providence intervened. The crusaders' grip on Toulouse was always precarious; it is likely that, after his return from Rome, Dominic discussed contingency arrangements to establish a base for his preachers outside Toulouse, including, very probably, the idea of trying to make a foundation in Paris – he had not forgotten Innocent's hopes, even if, for the moment, his brethren were only recognised as preachers in one diocese. But the crisis struck sooner than expected. He got wind of a plot to recapture Toulouse from Simon de Montfort; he also had a dream in which he foresaw Simon's death. He concluded that there was no time to lose. On 15 August he summoned the brethren and told them that they must split up without delay. A sizeable party was sent to Paris, including Bl. Bertrand of Garrigue, who had been prior of Saint Romain, with instructions to establish a community there, even though nothing had been done to prepare for their arrival; some of the friars were to study at the university. Their superior was Matthew of Paris, who was given the title of 'abbot', since Paris was to become the new motherhouse for the preachers; he was famously the 'first and last abbot', since the title was never used again in the order. At the same time four friars were sent to Spain to explore possibilities there. Dominic himself meanwhile would go back to the pope and try to secure his support for the expansion of the order precisely as a preaching order.

Dominic was taking a considerable risk. He had no guarantee that what he had achieved in Toulouse could be reproduced elsewhere. Outside the diocese of Toulouse, his brethren had no official status except that of canons regular, and, as such, they were subject to church laws incompatible with the apostolic ideals which he had espoused since 1206 and which were recognised as an essential part of their identity in Toulouse. And a radical divergence of opinion came to light almost at once. The brethren who went to Paris were, it seems, quite happy to adopt the normal way of life of canons; in their eyes, travelling on foot without money, begging their sustenance as they went, made sense as a tactic in the campaign against heresy, but had no relevance elsewhere. Dominic, by contrast, had discovered an aspect of the gospel in it; he wanted to embrace an even more radical poverty by renouncing all financial security for his communities. As he saw it, the link between preaching and poverty was an abiding ideal, learned, not just from the particular circumstances of the South of France, but from the model of Christ and his apostles. However there was no legal framework within which he could insist on this; all he could do was plead.

The scene now shifts to Italy. In the course of successive visits to the papal court, Dominic progressively won the pope over to his vision of a preaching order, following the model of the apostles and unrestricted by diocesan boundaries. On 11 February 1218, Honorius issued the first of several bulls recommending Dominic's preachers to all the prelates of the church; in it, for the first time, he used the phrase which was to become the name of the order, 'Order of Preachers'. By the end of April, he had added a clause to make it explicit that the order had its mandate to preach from the pope himself, and did not need any mandate from individual bishops. Before Dominic's death, Honorius had in effect reversed the decree of Lateran IV: instead of urging the bishops to seek the help of auxiliary preachers, he was summoning the bishops to assist the Order of Preachers.

Another crucial development occurred in the Spring of 1218. A French dean, Bl. Reginald of Orléans, arrived in Rome with his bishop; as he confided to Cardinal Ugolino, the future Pope Gregory IX, he was longing to abandon the world and devote himself to poverty and preaching. Quite independently of Dominic, quite independently of any campaign against heresy, he had found his own way to the same ideal as Dominic. Ugolino introduced them to each other, and Reginald, having been miraculously cured by Our Lady of a terrible sickness, made profession to Dominic.

While Dominic was in Rome, no doubt by arrangement, two of the brethren from Spain came to report to him and two from Paris. Together with some of his own travelling companions he sent them to make a foundation in Bologna. His policy is clear: it was from the great universities of Europe that he wanted his order to radiate. Reginald too was sent to Bologna, as Dominic's vicar. Whatever might be happening in Paris, at least the new community in Bologna would be shaped by someone who fully shared Dominic's own vision. And Reginald took the city by storm with his preaching; he attracted numerous vocations to the order, including some of the university's leading lights. Before long, they were able to start making foundations elsewhere in Italy: Florence, Bergamo, Milan, Verona, Piacenza and Brescia all had Dominican houses by the time Dominic died and they were all founded from Bologna.

Last, but not least, tidings arrived from Toulouse. Peter Seilhan and two others came to tell Dominic that Saint Romain seemed to be doomed. Simon de Montfort had been besieging the city in an attempt to recapture it, but without success. Having escaped, the three friars were unlikely to be able to return. Dominic accordingly asked the pope for a bull which would in effect substitute Prouille for Saint Romain as the official house of the order in the diocese.

There was no further reason to remain in Rome, except to celebrate Easter. Dominic had done much to further the development of his order and he had been busy as a preacher of God's word. Not least, he had made a point of visiting the nuns of Rome and offering what encouragement he could to the women who lived as solitaries, often in wretched conditions, in the old city walls. Now it was time to move on. Dominic decided to go to Spain.

Setting off with his party, on foot as always, Dominic first went to Bologna to visit his brethren there. Then he probably went to Narbonne, where his old friend, Arnaud was now archbishop; it seems likely that he left a few friars there to make a foundation. Toulouse was still under siege, so there was no point in trying to go there; Dominic and his companions went straight along the coast and down into Catalonia. As they travelled, Dominic talked about God to anyone who would listen to him. It was probably the first time he had ever encountered a significant Muslim population, but he was as willing to talk to them as to anyone else and to be friendly with them.

We have almost no information about Dominic's journey, but he seems to have made his way slowly West towards Castile; he picked up some recruits on the way and there was discussion with the Archbishop of Toledo about a possible foundation, though nothing came of it. At some stage Dominic received the news that Simon de Montfort had been killed and the siege of Toulouse abandoned. This obviously put a new complexion on the situation in the South of France; Dominic therefore sent some of his party to Paris, with instructions to tell Bertrand to return South and do whatever had to be done. He also sent Peter Seilhan to Paris, telling him that he was to make a foundation in Limoges, a good Catholic city, which had perhaps been recommended by Arnaud.

In due course, Dominic made contact with the brethren who had remained in Spain since 1217. They had acquired a site in Madrid, which was not yet a particularly important city; they had also attracted some women who wanted to be associated with them as nuns. Dominic himself received some of these women to profession and took the first steps towards forming them into a monastic community, with some brethren attached to it, as at Prouille. He then succeeded in establishing a community of brethren in Segovia.

We do not know how long Dominic stayed in the peninsula, but he appears to have picked an unfortunate time to revisit Toulouse. After Simon's death, the crusade was revived in 1219 under the leadership of Prince Louis of France, who resumed the siege of Toulouse. It looks as if Dominic arrived there in June to find that Saint Romain had, after all, not been lost, but that Prince Louis was expected any day with his army. Instead of having a leisurely discussion with Bertrand about the affairs of the order, Dominic had to move on almost at once. So he set off for Paris, taking Bertrand with him. On the way, they surprised some German pilgrims, who had taken it upon themselves to look after them, by suddenly bursting into fluent German, a miracle which Dominic refused to allow anyone to know about until after his death.

In Paris, the brethren had been given the use, but not yet the possession, of the hostel of Saint Jacques, and its proprietor, a professor in the university, was evidently willing to act as their lecturer in theology; but they were forced to keep a low profile – the local church authorities would not even allow them to celebrate the liturgy in public. They acquired a number of new recruits, but these were not of the same calibre as the people who were joining the order in Bologna. And they had settled down to behaving as respectable canons.

Two years had now passed since Dominic made his deal with William of Monferrato; he hoped that he would soon finish organising his order and that he would therefore be free to set off for some pagan land. With this in view, he received William into the order. He also discussed things with the brethren in Paris, but they gave him little joy. They would not hear of his suggestion that laybrothers should have full responsibility for the temporal administration of the order, nor do they seem to have responded with any enthusiasm to his plea that they should espouse mendicancy and the old apostolic ideals of the mission in the South.

While Dominic was in Paris, he received a visit from some-one who was destined to play a crucial rôle in the develop-ment of the order, Bl. Jordan of Saxony. Jordan was a Master of Arts and Bachelor of Theology in the university, and, though he was not yet even thinking of joining the order, he had taken a great interest in it and had started writing an account of its origins. He went to confession to Dominic and at his urging accepted ordination to the diaconate; he also heard Dominic tell the story of Reginald's miraculous cure and entry into the order. But one more thing was needed before his own vocation could become apparent.

Dominic was not the man to lose heart; he had a profound trust in God's providence, and never confused God's will with his own. Things would work out in the way God wanted, and that was all that mattered. So Dominic continued his journey, taking William with him. Their destination was the pope, to whom Dominic wished to report that the final step could now be taken in the shaping of the Order of Preachers: it was time for a general chapter to complete its constitutions. He and

William also wanted to declare their desire to go to some pagan land as missionaries.

On the way to the pope, Dominic naturally visited Bologna, and the thriving community he found there must have given him great pleasure. Most of the brethren had never seen him before, but they welcomed him as their father and founder. They had moved since Dominic was last there: thanks to the enthusiasm of Bl. Diana d'Andalò, they had been given the church of St Nicholas (later to become the church of San Domenico) which was on land belonging to her family. And their spirit had been formed by Reginald's almost fanatical belief in the combination of poverty and preaching. This was much more like what Dominic had been dreaming of. What was more, Diana was eager to establish a community of nuns under the brethren's auspices; soon after Dominic's arrival, she made her profession in his hands and promised to found a house of religious women belonging to the order.

Dominic was not a reserved man; while exhorting the brethren to be ardent preachers of the Word, he talked freely about his own plans to go and evangelise unbelievers, such as the Muslims he had met in Spain or the Cumans whose paganism had stirred the heart of Diego. If need be, he was eager to shed his blood for the gospel.

Seeing what Reginald had achieved in Bologna, Dominic decided to send him to Paris. Reginald, after all, had been a professor of canon law there, and he had known Abbot Matthew of old. Perhaps he would have more success in persuading the brethren there that mendicancy was not just an anti-heretical gimmick, but an evangelical and practical ideal even in Paris. Meanwhile, Dominic himself, with William, went on to see the pope.

At the papal court he found both joy and disappointment. While he was there, he received news that he was, no doubt, hoping and praying for: the brethren in Paris had decided to adopt mendicancy – it was this and the inspiration of Reginald which finally brought Jordan of Saxony into the order. There was now no serious obstacle left to impede the constitutional shaping of the whole order as an Order of Preachers committed to the model of Christ and his apostles, in poverty and dependence on the goodwill of others. The pope, for the first time, officially and explicitly recognised the existence of a single superior at the head of the whole order, and he gave Dominic special powers to complete its organisation at a general chapter; he also issued two bulls which, in effect, outlined what the church expected of the order, including a resounding endorsement of mendicancy. Dominic himself, however, was still not going to be free to realise his missionary aspirations.

Honorius III had inherited from his predecessor a project for the reform of the Roman nuns. There were several nunneries in Rome, but none of them was adequate to the needs of women with a serious monastic vocation; the plan was to build a new monastery at the church of San Sisto, and to invite all the nuns in the city to move there, under the care of the English order of Gilbertines, who specialised in this kind of work. But the building dragged on and there was no sign of any Gilbertines. So, in November 1219, Honorius asked

Dominic to see what he could do. Dominic therefore set about visiting the nuns to discover whether they would be willing to cooperate. Their response was generally negative, but two monasteries were interested, particularly that of Santa Maria in Tempulo. So Dominic apparently told the pope that the situation was not hopeless. Honorius then placed him in charge of the project and informed the Gilbertines that they were no longer wanted. Dominic, never afraid to think the unthinkable, toyed with the idea of closing Prouille and moving the monastery to Rome, nuns, friars and all; in the outcome, though, it was found sufficient to bring a few nuns from there to help. As a first move, Dominic established a community of brethren at San Sisto; in little over a year it was strong enough to launch a new foundation in Siena.

Instead of becoming a missionary to unbelievers, Dominic was obliged to oversee the erection of a monastery of nuns; but San Sisto was still a building-site so there was nothing to be done yet. Early in 1220, Dominic returned to Bologna, where he stayed for most of the year. The most important thing on his mind was the impending general chapter, due to begin a few days after Whitsun. As always he was not shy of letting people know what he was thinking, but his conversation now was about what he would like to see in the order's constitutions, not about pagans he hoped to convert.

SAINT DOMINIC RECEIVES WOMEN AT PROUILLE.

Later, Saint Dominic had responsibility for larger groups of nuns in Rome, Madrid and Bologna.

From a staind glass window in a Dominican convent in Tokyo, Japan, by Albert Carpentier, OP

CHAPTER FIVE

The Order of Preachers Comes to Maturity

UCH HAD happened in the four years since the order's birth. It had acquired a title, 'Order of Preachers', it had been given a universal mandate to exercise its function; once the brethren in Paris had agreed, it had received papal endorsement of mendicancy. It had a number of houses in France, Italy and Spain, and was already present in some places where formal houses would be established later. What it still lacked was a clear statement, embodied in law, of its structure, its system of government and its *modus operandi* as an Order of Preachers. It was the task of the 1220 general chapter to remedy this lack.

Dominic began the chapter by asking the brethren to 'depose' him. His position until then had been undisputed, but it would have been hard to give it any constitutional definition. Through all the stages that had turned an *ad hoc* anti-heretical mission in the South of France into a permanent, international, religious order, his had been the guiding hand; the one thing that had united the brethren, even when they seemed to be going in opposite directions, was their loyalty and obedience to him. But this gave him a personal rôle over the whole order, rather than an institutional rôle within it; this was underlined when the pope gave him special powers in preparation for the chapter. There is no occasion to doubt the genuineness of his humility, in suggesting that he was slack and unfit for duty; but asking to be deposed for these reasons was, in this period, the correct way for any ecclesiastical superior to offer his resignation. Dominic was, in effect, giving his brethren the chance, if they wanted, to choose a new head of the order, or, if they preferred, to reinstate him; but, if they chose the latter (as, of course, they did), instead of just having personal authority, he would be the first elected Master of the Order *within* the institution.

Even in 1216 it was realised that if the order expanded, as Innocent III wanted, it would in due course need to hold chapters, and that, as was suggested by a decree of Lateran IV, these would include provincial chapters; but in 1220 the order still had only rudimentary provincial structures, so, apart from a few details specific to general chapters, the capitulars formulated constitutions which could apply equally to general or provincial chapters.

They also gave legal form to the order's renunciation of properties and possessions. Henceforth all its houses would depend on alms.

Since the order as such had been given a universal mandate to preach by the pope, it was clearly important to determine how it transmitted this mandate to individual friars; this too was done in 1220. And since preachers needed to be properly educated, the chapter issued some rules about study and students.

Finally the order broke with tradition in making its primary structural unit the community, not the monastery; a Dominican community, defined as having at least twelve members, a prior and a teacher, could have legal existence even if it did not yet have any fixed abode.

The presence of the teacher *(doctor)* among the required ingredients for a formal community is striking. A Dominican house was not just to be a centre for preaching or a place where the order's own recruits could be trained; it was also to be a place of theological teaching. This was something Dominic himself believed in. During the summer of 1220 he received a visit from a friend he had made in the papal curia who had been sent as papal legate to the imperial chancellor, Conrad. Bishop of Metz, who was on his way to Rome for the emperor's coronation. It is no coincidence that, when Conrad returned to his diocese early in 1221, one of the first things he did was to encourage a Dominican foundation there in the hope that the brethren would benefit the laity by their preaching, and the clergy by their theology lectures. How did he know this was what he could expect from the order if he had not been told so by Dominic?

After the chapter, Dominic spent the rest of the year mostly in Bologna, except for two visits to Milan. An attempt to find a place for Diana's monastery was thwarted by the bishop, and Diana, impatient to become a nun, secretly received the habit in a nearby monastery of canonesses. Her family immediately removed her by force, injuring her in the process, and thereafter tried to ensure that she had no contact with the brethren, though Dominic managed to conduct a clandestine correspondence with her; it was not until 1223 that she finally got the Dominican nunnery she desired. The building of San

Sisto, however, was nearing completion; by December, it was time for Dominic to return to Rome.

There a shock awaited him: the nuns of Santa Maria in Tempulo had been talked out of moving to San Sisto by their friends and relations. But Dominic persuaded them to change their minds again, and, to protect them from further interference, he instituted strict enclosure. As the time approached for the nuns to enter San Sisto, the pope gave Dominic another place for the brethren, a family estate on the Aventine with the church of Santa Sabina. Most of the brethren went there, leaving only a few to look after the nuns, and, finally, on 28 February 1221, the nuns took possession of San Sisto, making profession in Dominic's hands as they entered. The first to do so was a young Roman woman, Bl. Cecilia, who was later sent to Bologna, where she would, in later years regale visitors with her memories of Dominic.

Having seen them into their new monastery, Dominic did not neglect the formation of his nuns; he visited them nearly every evening. But he began, once again, to dream of far off lands. On 29 March, he received a personal bull from the pope, recommending him, as head of the Order of Preachers, to all the prelates of the church; at much the same time, the pope wrote to all metropolitans bidding them select a few suitable religious and send them to him in view of a general mission to all the unbelievers still known to exist around the edges of Christendom. There can be little doubt that the pope intended Dominic to play an important part in this ambitious project.

By the beginning of May, it had evidently been decided where the Dominicans were to go, perhaps with Dominic at their head. The pope wrote to the King of Denmark and, for the first time, he commends the Dominicans not just as preachers of the Word, but also as evangelisers of unbelievers. This suggests that he wanted Dominic's friars to serve as apostles in Estonia, where the Danish king had recently made important conquests.

First, though, it was time for Dominic to return to Bologna for the second general chapter. In 1220, the order's essential legal framework had been constructed; the main item on the agenda in 1221 was its expansion into new territories. Dominicans were sent to England, where they soon established a house in Oxford, and to Hungary and Poland, possibly also to Greece. Two Scandinavian friars were already trying to make a foundation in Sweden, and in 1221 a party was sent with a Danish friar to take the pope's letter to the King of Denmark. The order was all set to become a powerful force for the preaching of the gospel.

Dominic himself, however, seems to have had a premonition that he was soon to die, although he was still in surprisingly good health; he said as much to some students whom he had befriended in Bologna. Nevertheless he set off after the chapter to make his leisurely way to Venice, preaching and begging his bread as he went. But by the end of July, when he returned to Bologna, he was a very sick man. He died on 6 August 1221, and was buried in the church of the brethren.

The brethren had not forgotten his enthusiasm for the

conversion of unbelievers. Within a few years of his death, they had embarked on missions to the Muslims, the Cumans, the Prussians, the pagans in the Ukraine and the Estonians and then began to go even further afield. They were also quickly involved in attempts to bring oriental Christians back into communion with Rome.

Dominic was venerated as a saint from the time of his death. but no steps were taken to get him canonised until 1233. In that year, his remains were translated to a new, more worthy, tomb, and a formal process of canonisation initiated. He was declared a saint by Gregory IX on 3 July 1234.

SAINT DOMINIC MEDITATING IN PRAYER

'And his stance was as if he were reading very reverently and with devotion before God. He seemed then to be meditating in prayer on the words of God and, as it were, to be telling himself of them lovingly.' *Modi Orandi Sancti Dominici.*

Detail from number five of the *Ways of Prayer of Saint Dominic.*

Chapter Six

The Character of Dominic

IT IS OFTEN said that saints are difficult to live with; judging from the testimony of people who knew him well, Dominic was easy to live with. Although he was readily moved to tears, either by the wonders of God's gifts or by the distress of his fellow men, he was always cheerful. He could be a stern disciplinarian, but he was always affable and companionable, totally sincere, but devoid of all pompous earnestness. He made people feel trusted; they knew they were genuinely free to disagree with him or, for that matter, to have their little jokes with him. He expected everyone to give themselves without stint; but he appreciated that they could only do so if they had space in which to discover their own strengths and weaknesses and the particular gifts and graces they had from God. This is why he declared that the rules of the order were merely human rules – there was no sin involved in breaking them; he even said that if he thought religious rules were being taken in any other way, he would personally destroy them all with his knife. For the same reason, the order, probably in 1220, introduced a revolutionary new principle into religious life: since the order was founded primarily to be of service to souls, any of the brethren could be dispensed at any time from any traditional monastic observance for the sake of study, preaching or anything else. To be effective students, preachers, teachers or whatever other function they might have in the order, they needed to be able to take responsibility for themselves; a holy cage might make it easier to avoid temptation, but it would not make them good Dominicans.

Dominic emphasised the importance of study; that was why he systematically sent his friars to the great university centres. But the order was not meant to consist solely of academics. Preachers needed to be properly instructed, but, above all, they needed a deep and vivid faith in God and a readiness to let the Holy Spirit enlighten their words and deeds. Assuring them of his prayers, he sent even young priests out to preach, before they felt ready for the task, bidding them trust in God to give them the right words to speak.

Dependence on God is the key to the whole thing. Dominic told his brethren that they should be always speaking either about God or with God, and that is how he lived himself. Prayer was not a spiritual exercise, to be performed primly at the proper times, it was a constant need to cry out to God, the source of all blessing, for his own needs, the needs of his brethren, the needs of sinners and unbelievers, the needs of the whole world. Dominic used to spend most of the night in prayer, and he prayed so noisily that he disturbed the brethren with his roaring and bellowing – that is no doubt one reason why the constitutions instructed novice masters to teach their novices how to pray quietly!

While he was travelling, if he was not speaking about God, Dominic would pray and meditate, often singing hymns as he went; sometimes he would say to his companions, 'Let us think about our Saviour.' He was devoted to the bible and always carried St Matthew's gospel and the epistles of St Paul with him, and he encouraged his followers to be eager students of God's Word. According to the early constitutions, novices must be exhorted to be 'always reading something or thinking about something'. Dominic was a believer in using time profitably as the occasion presented itself, rather than in trying to make time for things by legislation or rigid discipline.

'I never knew anyone,' declared one of his companions 'whose service of God I liked so much. And he was more zealous for the salvation of souls than any man I ever saw.' 'He was loved by everyone rich and poor, Jew and infidel,' according to another of them.

As he lay dying Dominic tried to comfort his brethren with the assurance 'I shall be more useful to you where I am going,' and he lived up to his word. In later years Peter Seilhan liked to say that, in all his troubles, he had always invoked Dominic, and he had never once been let down.

In one sense, the life of Dominic in this world ended in August 1221, though his memory lives on in the hearts of his family of friars and nuns, sisters and laity. But in another sense, the world still hears his voice, even if it does not recognise it as his. As St Catherine of Siena says, 'The voice of Dominic's preaching is still heard today and will continue to be heard' in the preaching of his followers. The great idea which Dominic launched in his lifetime confronts men and women in the church and far beyond the limits of the church in the works of people like St Thomas Aquinas (whom even the unsympathetic Charles Lamb called 'Honest Tom of Aquin'), St Albert the Great, St Catherine of Siena, Bl. Fra Angelico, Savonarola, Meister Eckhart, Bartolomé de las Casas, St Martin de Porres and a host of others who have in their different ways influenced the life and thought and piety of the church and of the world.

SAINT DOMINIC 'WOULD OPEN SOME BOOK'

'Sitting there quietly and readied by the sign of the cross, he would open some book ... and he would read and be as moved in mind as if he were hearing the Lord speaking...'

Detail from number eight of the *Ways of Prayer of St Dominic*.

Books for further study

W. A. Hinnebusch, *The Dominicans, a Short History*, New York 1975, Dublin 1980; Vladimir J. Koudelka, *Dominic,* London 1997; Simon Tugwell *The Way of the Preacher*, London 1979; Simon Tugwell, *Early Dominicans* (Classics of Western Spirituality) New York.